Exploring Plants

by
Rebecca Olien

SCHOLASTIC
PROFESSIONAL BOOKS

NEW YORK • TORONTO • LONDON • AUCKLAND • SYDNEY

For my daughter Jessica

Cover illustration and design by Jaime Lucero
Interior design by Solutions By Design, Inc.
Interior illustrations by Kate Flanagan

ISBN # 0-590-96372-4
Copyright © 1997 by Rebecca Olien
All rights reserved.
Printed in the U.S.A.

12 11 10 9 8 7 6 5 4 3 2 1   7 8 9/9/01/0

CONTENTS

Introduction

In all their various forms, plants surround us with possibilities for exploration, experimentation, and discovery.

In my experience as a classroom teacher, I have learned that my students learn best from their encounters with plant life by being actively involved. The activities in this book provide opportunities for children to observe, experiment, and respond to plants through a hands-on format. Whether discovering the miniature plant in a bean seed, tracking the transformation of speck-sized seeds as they grow into full-sized plants, or preparing a food grown in the classroom, children will engage in exciting sensory learning.

The activities and projects in this book also encourage students to ask questions. Inquiry becomes a catalyst for further investigation and higher-level thinking, and you'll find special critical thinking questions throughout these pages.

An important component of this book is the Science Journal. You'll find ideas for getting started on page 6. By setting up these journals at the beginning of your plant study and using them throughout, students will create an excellent learning and evaluative tool.

Integrating science teaching with other disciplines helps students reinforce their learning. Each section includes ideas for relating your plant study to other curriculum areas. You'll also find suggestions for quality children's literature to use with your projects.

In addition to whole-class projects, I have included activities in which children can work alone, with partners, in small groups, or at home. This gives all children a mixture of settings and a chance to

learn independently, or to work on cooperative skills. I hope that these activities will open the eyes and minds of your students to the wonderful and extraordinary world of plants!

—*Rebecca Olien*

CHAPTER ONE

GETTING STARTED

What do students already know about plants? What would they like to find out? What do you think they should learn? The activities in this chapter will help you determine the answers to these questions.

The Science Journal

Writing helps students sort out ideas, record information, form questions, and evaluate their learning. A journal provides a personal place in which students can respond to and reflect upon science activities. A journal can be a loose-leaf notebook to which students add pages as needed, or a collection of the reproducibles from this book. (To make their own Science Journals, students can fold a 12-by-18-inch sheet of oak tag in half, punch holes down the folded side, add pages, and put together with brass fasteners or bind with string.) You'll find a basic reproducible Science Journal page on page 8 as well as recording pages for specific lessons throughout the book. Young students, or those with special needs, can use invented spelling, drawings, and dictated descriptions in their journals, while older students can draw detailed diagrams of their observations and write more thorough explanations. Science Journals are an excellent place for students to track the progress of different kinds of plants growing in your classroom. (See Chapter 2, Getting Green, for more.) Students can measure and graph growth rates, and observe and record differences between different kinds of plants, such as leaf shape and

quantity, colors, and other attributes. Science Journals provide an important learning tool for children at all levels.

A Science Journal also helps you as the teacher to observe what concepts a student grasps, to see what information is missing, or to determine what facts are misunderstood. Throughout the book, you'll find critical thinking questions which you can present for students to respond to in their journals. As students learn to ask their own questions, they can respond to these in their journals as well.

As a beginning journal activity, try one or more of the following:

※ Create a **KWL** (**K**now—**W**ant to Know—**L**earned) chart with the class. Students might take turns adding to one posted on a bulletin board. They can then copy it into their journals. Encourage students to add to and revise this chart throughout your plant study.

※ Have children draw a picture of a plant. Ask them to label any parts they know.

※ Give each child a stone, then ask: *Is this a plant? How do you know?* Encourage students to give as many reasons as they can.

※ Have children make a list of any plant names they know.

※ Ask: *What does a plant need to live?* Have children answer in a list or a labeled picture.

※ Ask: *Where can a plant live?* Have children draw or cut out pictures from magazines to show different places.

※ Ask: *What things do people use that come from plants?* Have children make a list or draw pictures of their ideas.

At the end of the unit, have students return to these questions to add to or change their responses. By marking changes in colored pencil, both you and your students can easily see what learning has taken place.

Name_____

My Science Journal

We are learning about _____

_____

My prediction: _____

_____

To find out more, I _____

_____

_____

My observations: _____

_____

_____

My conclusions: _____

_____

_____

Playground Plant Search

It's always a good idea to start teaching with the familiar. In this activity, students discover plants that grow in your school yard and share the names of those they know.

MATERIALS   ❊ Science Journals, pencils

WHAT TO DO   . . . .

1 Explain that the class is going on a plant hunt. Ask students what kinds of plants they think they will see on school grounds. Accept any possibilities as to which are plants; use this initial discussion to get students thinking about what a plant is. Then ask: *Where are the most likely places to find plants on the school grounds? Are there any plants growing on the blacktop or cement areas?*

2 Proceed to the playground with Science Journals and pencils.

3 Stop as the first plant is spotted and ask what kind of plant it is. Have students write down the plant name or draw a quick picture of it. Can students see any more of the same plant nearby? If so, have them indicate this with a tally mark next to their entries. Students can also make tally marks next to the picture.

4 Choose students to lead the class to other plants, following the same procedure.

5 Finally, go to the areas on the school grounds where students did *not* think plants could grow. Often you'll find moss, grass, or other hearty plant types pushing through cracks, or growing along blacktop edges.

6 Return to the classroom to compare and share the information. Work with students to record the results on a chart or bar graph.

7 Discuss the results of the plant search with the class. Were there any surprises? In conclusion, have students close their journals and try to remember the names of the plants that grow on their playground.

Plant Products Matchup Game

In this activity, students learn some of the many ways in which people depend on plants.

MATERIALS   ❊ Plants and Products reproducibles (pages 12 and 13) for each student, scissors

WHAT TO DO

1. Cut apart the plant and product pictures, and provide each student with a set.

2. Have children discuss in small groups how they think the pictures match. Children can pair their own pictures as the discussion takes place.

3. Discuss the results with the class. Ask: *Which pairs were the easiest to match? Which ones were guesses? What clues did you use?* Give information so that students match the pictures correctly. (*coconut/palm tree; pumpkin/pumpkin vine; sunflower seeds/ sunflower; sugar in bag/sugarcane; paper/pine tree; baseball bat/hickory tree; maple syrup in jug/maple tree; bread/wheat plant; shirt/cotton plant; cherry/cherry tree*)

4. Have students mix up their pictures and try to sort them again on their own. Afterward, have students check one another's work.

5. Use the pictures to play a game of concentration during the next class period. (See the activity below.)

TEACHER TIP
To make the cards sturdier, paste them on oak tag before cutting them apart.

Plant Products Concentration Game

MATERIALS   ❊ Plants and Products cards (from reproducible pages 12 and 13)

WHAT TO DO

1. Break the class up into pairs. Have them mix up the plant and product cards, and place them facedown in rows.

2. Taking turns, students choose two cards to see if they have a match. If not, they turn the cards back over in the same spots. If there is a match, students keep the pair in front of them.

3. The game is over when all cards have been matched. The player with the most cards wins.

TEACHER TIP
You can modify this game by using fewer pairs of cards.

Mystery Plants

Mystery plants make a great weekly activity in which you give one clue each day. You can also give all the clues at one time.

MATERIALS   ❀ Mystery Plants and Clues reproducible (page 14), Science Journals

WHAT TO DO

1 Give clues to selected plants one at a time throughout the day or week. Suggest that students copy these into their journals along with their guesses. As each clue is given, questions may arise on word meaning. Explaining what these vocabulary words mean helps provide informal background for the rest of the unit.

2 Record students' guesses on a master list.

3 After you have given the last clue, have students reread all the clues and make a final guess.

4 Reveal the mystery plant's identity.

TEACHER TIP
You can modify this activity by giving students a selected list of plants to guess from, or by displaying pictures of all the mystery plants for the class to choose from.

Critical Thinking Questions

ASK: *Which questions made it easy or hard to guess?*
       What other clues would be helpful?

Plants and Products

Product
coconut

Plant
palm tree

Product
pumpkin

Plant
pumpkin vine

Product
sunflower seeds

Plant
sunflower

Product
sugar

Plant
sugarcane

Product
paper

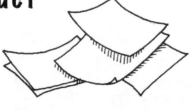

Plant
pine tree

Plants and Products

Product
baseball bat

Plant
hickory tree

Product
maple syrup

Plant
maple tree

Product
bread

Plant
wheat plant

Product
shirt

Plant
cotton plant

Product
cherry

Plant
cherry tree

Mystery Plants and Clues

MYSTERY PLANT NO. 1

Clue: This mystery plant is a tall plant, but it is not a tree.

Clue: It has big heart-shaped leaves.

Clue: Its flower is very big and has yellow petals.

Clue: Birds, squirrels, and people eat the seeds of this plant.

Mystery Plant: *sunflower*

MYSTERY PLANT NO. 2

Clue: The leaves on this plant are grouped by threes.

Clue: You should never touch this plant.

Clue: This plant is sometimes called "itch weed."

Clue: The leaves turn red in the fall

Mystery Plant: *poison ivy*

MYSTERY PLANT NO. 3

Clue: This plant floats in water.

Clue: It has large round leaves.

Clue: Frogs sometimes sit on the leaves of this plant.

Clue: It has a big yellow flower.

Mystery Plant: *lily pad*

MYSTERY PLANT NO. 4

Clue: This plant grows in warm soil.

Clue: People dig up part of this plant to eat.

Clue: A favorite sandwich filling comes from this plant.

Clue: You can buy the seed of this plant at baseball games.

Mystery Plant: *peanut*

MYSTERY PLANT NO. 5

Clue: Gardeners grow this plant for food.

Clue: It has feathery leaves.

Clue: Horses like this plant.

Clue: It has a bright orange root.

Mystery Plant: *carrot*

MYSTERY PLANT NO. 6

Clue: The seeds of this plant are held in cones.

Clue: People decorate this plant during certain holidays.

Clue: It has needles.

Clue: The needles are flat and short.

Mystery Plant: *pine tree*

MYSTERY PLANT NO. 7

Clue: This plant grows near water.

Clue: It has a square stem.

Clue: This plant helps flavor toothpaste.

Clue: You can taste this plant in candy canes.

Mystery Plant: *peppermint*

MYSTERY PLANT NO. 8

Clue: This plant is a tree with a short name.

Clue: The wood of this tree burns well in a fireplace.

Clue: Squirrels like this tree.

Clue: Its seeds are called acorns.

Mystery Plant: *oak tree*

MYSTERY PLANT NO. 9

Clue: This plant has a bright yellow flower.

Clue: It sends out seeds that float like parachutes.

Clue: People call this plant a weed.

Clue: It has a hollow stem.

Mystery Plant: *dandelion*

MYSTERY PLANT NO. 10

Clue: This plant grows on a vine.

Clue: People make pies with its large orange fruit.

Clue: People eat the seeds of this plant.

Clue: Children carve this plant's fruit on Halloween.

Mystery Plant: *pumpkin*

Plant Connections

Display a collection of numbered pictures and objects on a bulletin board, some of which come from plants, and some of which don't. On a banner across the top write the question: WHICH OF THESE COME FROM PLANTS? Provide numbered slips of paper for students to check off the items they think come from plants. Encourage them to reevaluate their answers as they discover new information throughout the unit. When everyone has had a chance to respond, add labels next to each object or picture on the display to tell what plant or nonplant source it came from.

Examples for pictures or objects that come from plants: cotton balls, rubber bands, paper, perfume, dried fruit, a wooden spoon, a cork, a pencil.

Examples of objects which don't come from plants: a metal spoon, a wool sock, a plastic bag, pennies, glasses.

EXTENSION As a follow-up, ask students to find a picture of their own to add to the bulletin board. Stress that students must know whether or not the item comes from a plant. Set aside time for the class to discuss the new pictures.

LITERATURE CONNECTION

In *Pierrot's ABC Garden* by Anita Lobel, children practice saying and learning plant names. Invite students to make a class alphabet book, choosing different plant names for as many letters as possible.

CHAPTER TWO

GETTING GREEN

To study plants effectively, students need access to live samples. The best way to do this is to grow them in your classroom. Here are some suggestions for an easy-to-manage planting station. You and your class will have fun adding your own ideas as well.

Creating a Planting Station

There's no way around it, planting is messy! You can minimize this mess by preparing your planting area ahead of time. Choose a corner or area away from the main traffic flow in your room. If possible, use a table or counter close to a sink. Make sure the surface area is sturdy and at a comfortable height for students. Cover the work surface and area below it with large plastic leaf bags or an old tarp or shower curtain.

Soil Plants grow best in soil that provides a light crumbly texture, good drainage, and high nutrient value. Rather than mixing soil for each planting, prepare a large batch to store and use as needed. A standard potting soil recipe is equal parts of sand, garden soil, and peat moss (or humus). You can find these ingredients at gardening stores. Mix them together in a child's wading pool or on a tarp, stirring with a small hoe or broom handle. Use a plastic garbage can as a sturdy storage bin. You can create scoops from milk jugs or other large plastic containers.

Containers Stock shelves or boxes near the work area with a supply of planting containers. Don't feel limited to commercial pots; dishpans, fish bowls, milk jugs, plastic bottles, wooden boxes, and beach pails work just as well. You can adapt containers by punching holes in the bottom or lower sides for drainage. You can use glass or stiff plastic without holes if you place a 2-inch layer of gravel in the bottom before adding soil. To personalize the containers, have children decorate clay or plastic pots with permanent markers or paint designs on wooden boxes. A variety of planters will add interest to your classroom garden.

If table space is limited, try hanging planters. You might also rig up simple wood shelves hung with rope to hold some of your classroom garden.

If your classroom is on the ground floor, consider having a movable garden. Add casters to barrels or wooden boxes to make them mobile. Or place your plant containers on wheeled carts or wagons to transport them outdoors when the weather is favorable.

Light Place your plants near windows when possible. To increase the amount of light or to give needed light where there are no windows, you can use fluorescent fixtures. Incandescent bulbs give off a lot of heat and do not emit enough variety in wavelengths. Plants generally need 12 to 14 hours of light, so if you are depending on electric lights, set up a timer for after-school hours and weekends. Use lamps with bendable "goose necks" or hang lights on chains or pulleys that you can adjust to plant height. Most plants do well with lights placed 6 to 8 inches above them.

Water Children are often too enthusiastic when it comes to watering plants. Overwatering causes mildew and root rot. (Students will discover this through firsthand experience!)

To avoid this problem, set up a watering schedule each week. Teach students this simple test: poke a finger into the soil up to the middle knuckle. If the soil is dry, then the plant can use more water. Provide watering cans that students can handle. Smaller cans that pour a narrow stream of water work best in young children's hands.

What to Grow

By growing a variety of plants, you'll encourage interest and curiosity. You'll also have many of the plants that you need for the activities in this book.

Plants for Vegetables with shallow root systems and short germination periods work
Food well in a classroom garden. Try growing leafy cool-weather plants such as

lettuce, chard, spinach, and kale. Radish seeds, which you'll need for the activity on page 29, are quick to germinate and grow. Lima beans are easy to sprout, as are alfalfa seeds, soybeans, mustard, cress, and mung beans (see Chapter 4, Germination). Cherry tomatoes need larger pots and more light, but are easy to raise. Other vegetables that do well in medium-sized containers (8-inch pots) are finger carrots, green onions, and pixie tomatoes. You might also include herbs such as parsley, basil, thyme, and savory in your classroom garden. Safety Note: Check the information on seed packets to make sure that the seeds you bring in for children to handle have not been treated with chemicals. See *Classroom Resources*, page 72, for suppliers that sell organic seeds.

GROWING HERBS INDOORS	
Herb	Days to Germinate
basil	5 to 10
catnip	4
chives	7
cress	7
parsley	20 or more
summer savory	5
thyme	20 or more

Part of the fun of growing food is eating the harvest. With adult supervision, students can chop vegetables in a food processor and mix them with softened cream cheese to make a cracker spread. They can hang herbs to dry and then crumble them into herb butter or use them on a cheese pizza. Students might also feed leftover vegetables to school pets.

Plants for Flowers   To grow flowers successfully in your classroom, try short nonspreading varieties such as alyssums, zinnias, asters, nasturtiums, geraniums, and snapdragons. These, as well as other annuals, are easy and quick to grow. Many flowers, such as marigolds and phlox, are available in dwarf varieties that work well in containers. Other plants, including fuchsias, petunias, begonias, and impatiens adapt to hanging containers. You can use your classroom flowers in the activities in Chapter 6, Flowers.

Terrariums   Terrariums are wonderful examples of miniature plant communities. Find local plants to create small replicas of forest, field, bog, or desert environments. Create nonnative environments with plants purchased in nurseries.

You can use any wide-mouthed clear plastic or glass container for a terrarium. Pickle jars, mayonnaise jars, goldfish bowls, canning jars, or candy bowls will all work. You don't need drainage holes; instead, layer the bottom of the container with an inch of coarse sand, gravel, or clay-pot shards. Over this material sprinkle a layer of charcoal (available at pet stores or gardening centers). These two layers provide drainage and help purify the contents of the terrarium. For the top, add 2 inches of soil (the same mixture used for other plantings). The soil material should fill a fourth of the available space.

To plant, you will need tools that can reach down into the small spaces of your container. Kitchen tongs, basters, chopsticks, and skewers work well. You can also fashion tongs by taping craft sticks to tweezers and bending heavy wire to form long-handled hooks. Invite the children to plan how to arrange the plants. Demonstrate how to make a hole in the soil with a chopstick or a piece of wire. Then help students gently remove excess soil from roots, press the roots into a ball, and use tongs to lower each plant into a hole. Students can landscape their terrarium with rocks, twigs, and shells.

Maintaining a terrarium is relatively simple. Place it in indirect sunlight or under a fluorescent light. Water the terrarium sparingly with a baster or eyedropper. Your terrarium will need about one or two teaspoons of water per plant every three to four weeks. Keep the soil moist but not soggy. Cover the terrarium with plastic wrap and secure with a rubber band to ensure a high humidity level. If the soil dries out, add more water. If the inside fogs with condensation, poke holes in the cover to provide ventilation. Trim the plants as they grow beyond their space, and remove dead leaves.

If students are making a desert terrarium, they should mix the top layer of soil with additional sand and use small stones, pebbles, or marble chips to decorate around the plants. Since succulents and cacti need arid conditions, students can leave the container open and place their desert terrarium in full sunlight.

For still another variation to your miniature plant habitats, grow water plants in an aquarium. Set up the aquarium as you would for fish; in fact, students may want to include fish in the plan. Be sure the aquarium gravel is mixed with iron-rich clay and fertilization tablets. Purchase plants such as anacharis, Amazon sword, and corkscrew vallesneria at a pet store. You might also be able to collect native plants from a local pond. Model how to remove the soil from each plant and simply push it into the gravel. Keep the aquarium away from sunlight to discourage overheating and algae growth.

LITERATURE CONNECTION

As children learn how to take care of classroom plants, they will enjoy the book *The Pumpkin Man and the Crafty Creeper* by Margaret Mahy. This humorous story describes a man who happily grows pumpkins until he begins taking care of a creeper plant that not only demands fulfillment of basic needs, but also requires constant entertainment. After reading this story, discuss what the creeper needed to live and what it did not need.

CHAPTER THREE

SEEDS

Before introducing the following seed activities, ask students to write in their Science Journals a definition of what they think a seed is and does. Encourage students to revise or add to their definitions as they complete activities on seeds.

All Sorts of Seeds

Seeds come in an amazing variety of sizes, shapes, and textures. By handling and sorting different seed types, students will recognize similarities and differences between common seeds as they also develop classification skills.

MATERIALS

✿ for each student: a handful of seeds (cooking seeds such as dried pinto, navy, or lima beans; dried corn; peas; sunflower seeds; rice; and popcorn kernels), paper, paper cups, crayons, Science Journal

WHAT TO DO

1 Give each student a cup containing a mixture of seeds.

2 Have students draw six big circles on their paper.

3 Ask students to explore ways to sort their seeds into the circles. Explain that they do not need to use *all* the circles.

4 Stop and share the different types of groupings students have tried.

5 Take one student idea at a time and have the rest of the class sort seeds this way; for instance, by color.

6 Next, have students write labels for each of their groups and place these next to or inside the circles. You can premake labels for younger students so they can choose which ones to use.

7 Ask students to mix their seeds together and sort them again using a different criterion, perhaps texture, seed-coat patterns, or size.

TEACHER TIP
You can also use seeds found outdoors, such as maple seeds or acorns, to add variety to the activity.

Critical Thinking Questions

ASK: What makes the popcorn seeds different from the others?

How do these seeds feel when you rub them through your hands?

These seeds have marks on them; how can we label their group?

8 Have students make labels to go with these new groups.

9 Conclude by asking students to write in their Science Journals about the different properties of seeds they identified during the sorting activity.

Seed Bingo

To help the class distinguish among different kinds of seeds, create this seed bingo game. Students can play it in groups of four or five.

MATERIALS   ❊ 8-by-10-inch tag-board rectangles (one for each student player), marker, ruler, a variety of different seeds, clean empty cans to hold seeds

WHAT TO DO

1 With a ruler, draw lines dividing each tag-board card into nine spaces. Write FREE in the center square and write the names of seeds in the other squares. Do this randomly so that the cards are not exactly the same.

maple	pea	kidney bean
popcorn	FREE	maple
acorn	sunflower	lima bean

sunflower	lima bean	acorn
popcorn	FREE	pea
kidney bean	sunflower	lima bean

2 Review with the class the names of the seeds you are using. Display each seed so students can examine it.

3 Model a round of the game before students play on their own. Draw a seed from a can and call out the seed's name. Hold the seed so that children can see its shape.

4 Explain that players then choose this kind of seed from their cups and place it on the corresponding space of their bingo card. The first player to fill the card with seeds wins.

Seed-Pattern Pencil Holders

In this activity, students make patterned pencil holders. Creating patterns with seeds provides an opportunity to informally experience the differences and similarities in seed texture, shape, and color.

MATERIALS   ✿ mixture of seeds; glue; empty, clean cans from soup or vegetables; colored construction paper; Science Journals

WHAT TO DO ·

1 To begin, have students cover the outside of a can with a piece of construction paper. Then they glue the paper around the can.

2 Next, challenge students to create repeating patterns with seeds on another piece of paper. They should keep these fairly simple.

3 Students then carefully glue seeds on the holder, row by row, to create their pattern. Then they set the holder aside so it can dry.

4 Follow up by having students draw their seed patterns in their Science Journals.

LITERATURE CONNECTIONS

Use traditional stories to add a literary dimension to your seed study. Children enjoy retelling or acting out "Jack and the Beanstalk" and "The Little Red Hen." You might also read the folktale *Bean Boy* by George Shannon about a boy who learns to take care of himself by using his beans.

Seed Surprises

To foster additional curiosity, bring in fruits which were not identified as seed-bearing by students. Possibilities might include bananas, avocados, papayas, seeded grapes, pomegranates, and coconuts (which are seeds).

MATERIALS

❊ fruits mentioned above, plus oranges, apples, lemons; knife; 8-by-8-inch (or larger) paper squares; crayons

WHAT TO DO

1. Hold up each fruit, one at a time, and help identify it if necessary. Ask students to describe what type of seeds they think might be inside. Ask questions about size, number, and color.

2. Cut open each fruit to display the seed or seeds inside. Ask: *Which seeds were surprises? Why?* (Some students may be surprised that the tiny black specks in a banana are seeds, or by the amount of seeds in a pomegranate, or by the size of the avocado seed.)

3. Share samples of the fruits for tasting. Select seeds to be planted and labeled by helpers at the planting station.

4. Follow up by having students make "seed surprises" of their own. Have them fold the square pieces of paper into four smaller squares. Students should then draw diagonal lines through each small square as shown. In each of the center triangles students can draw or paste a picture of a fruit. They should write the name of this fruit in the corresponding outside triangle. After folding over the outside triangles, have students glue on a seed for each fruit pictured.

   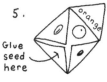

Critical Thinking Questions

ASK: *Which fruit could start the most new plants?*

Do fruits with small seeds have more seeds than fruits with large seeds?

EXTENSIONS

❊ Incorporate math concepts by counting seeds. Make a bar graph showing how many seeds are in each fruit. Ask: Which fruits have an equal number of seeds? Which fruit has the most seeds? The least?

❊ Compare seed sizes by asking: Which seeds are smallest? Largest? Have students glue seeds onto a strip of paper according to size.

Moving On

To survive, a plant needs a place to grow. Seeds travel from parent plants to new places in different ways. You can describe these methods of dispersal in the following ways:

Grabbers: seeds with little hooks or sticky substances which help them cling to animal fur and people's clothes;

Floaters: seeds that float in water to new locations;

Wind Drifters: seeds that glide easily in a breeze;

Spinners: seeds with wings that propel them with a spin to the ground.

By testing and classifying seeds based on the way they move, students can learn about the different adaptations seeds have for dispersal.

MATERIALS ❄ a variety of different seeds (milkweed seeds, dandelion parachutes, cockleburs, pussy willows, sycamore seeds, maple seeds, acorns); paper plates labeled GRABBER, FLOATER, WIND DRIFTER, AND SPINNER; scraps of craft fur, wool sock or mitten, or stuffed animal toys; straws; cups or bowls for water; Science Journals

WHAT TO DO

1 Assign students to groups of three. Ask students what might happen if seeds all fell in one place and tried to grow. (*They would be too crowded and would not get what they need in order to grow.*) Explain that students will do some tests to find out how seeds travel.

2 Model how to do each test and how to sort the seeds on the labeled plates according to the test results.

SEED TESTS:

Grabber Test: Press a piece of fuzzy material or a stuffed animal toy on top of the seed. If it sticks, place the seed on the grabber plate.

Floater Test: Place the seed in water. If the seed floats, place it on the floater plate.

Wind Drifter Test: Blow on the seed gently with a straw. If the seed moves across a desk or table, place it on the wind drifter plate.

Spinner Test: Hold the seed above your head and drop it. If the seed spins as it falls, place it on the spinner plate.

3 As students complete the tests, have them write the results in their Science Journals. Then instruct them to glue the seeds to their plates. Share and compare the results among the groups. Discuss any differences.

Design a Seed Traveler

Use this activity as a creative extension of how seeds travel and as a way to incorporate critical thinking into the lesson.

MATERIALS ❋ paper clips; materials to make seed travelers (balloons, plastic wrap, thread, Styrofoam, tinfoil, paper, tape, cotton); Science Journals

WHAT TO DO

1 Show the class a paper clip. Tell students to imagine that the paper clip is a seed from a paper-clip tree. Ask: *How might the paper-clip seed travel to a new place so it can grow?*

2 After generating a few ideas, have students work in small groups. Explain that students can add parts—fins, tails, wings—or modify the paper clip in other ways so that it is a good traveler. For example, to make a wind traveler, ask students to figure out how they can make it glide (attach it to a paper airplane or a parachute). For a floater, have them think about ways to make the paper clip float in water (make a Styrofoam or tinfoil boat; tape the paper clip to a blown-up balloon). For a seed that grabs, students must devise ways to make the paper clip stick to things it touches (add a rolled piece of tape or Velcro).

TEACHER TIP
Students might create a paper-clip tree on which to display their seed-traveler designs.

3 Have students share their completed seed adaptations with the class. Ask each team to describe or demonstrate how their paper-clip seed has become a better traveler. Then have students write up this activity in their Science Journals.

What's Inside a Seed?

By taking apart large lima beans, students find all the parts necessary for a new plant to grow.

MATERIALS ❀ dried lima beans, soaked overnight in water; hand lenses; Science Journals

WHAT TO DO

1 Explain that lima beans purchased in a grocery store are hard and must be cooked until they are soft enough to eat. The seeds that students will use have been soaked so that they are soft enough to take apart.

2 Pass out three or four seeds to each student.

3 Ask students to observe carefully as you demonstrate how to slip off the outside layer of a seed. Have students remove the outside layer of a seed in the same way. Call on volunteers to describe what this layer looks and feels like. Explain that this outside layer is called the seed coat. Ask: *Why might the seed need a coat?* (protection)

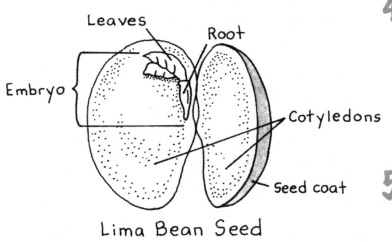

Leaves

Root

Embryo

Cotyledons

Seed coat

Lima Bean Seed

4 Show students how to split the seed in half along the crack. Have them open the broad, rounded side to avoid damaging the plant structures within. Point out that inside the seed is a baby plant called an embryo. Invite students to take a closer look with a hand lens.

5 Ask volunteers to describe the parts (two leaves and a root) visible in the embryo. Have students draw and label diagrams and record in their Science Journals observations about the seeds.

TEACHER TIP
You may wish to follow up this exploration with the germination activity on page 33.

6 Explain that in order to grow, an embryo needs food. Ask students where they think the seed's food is stored (in the big sides of the seed called the *cotyledons*). Ask students what else they think seeds need in order to grow into bean plants. (Air, moisture, and nutrients from the soil once their built-in food store is used up.)

Seed Read

This activity helps students learn about the cultivation of seeds and gives them practice in reading directions.

MATERIALS ❊ Radish Seed Package reproducible (page 30), bunch of radishes, radish seeds, dishpans of soil for each group, rulers, overhead projector (if available), Science Journals

WHAT TO DO

1 Show the class a bunch of radishes and explain that students will learn how to grow them. Assign students to work in groups.

2 Display the radish seeds and provide each group with a copy of the reproducible. Make another copy to use on an overhead projector.

3 Using the overhead, guide students in reading the "seed package." Teach unfamiliar vocabulary words as you go.

4 Copy the following questions on a chart. Then have each group work together to use their seed packages to answer the questions.

1. How far apart should you plant the seeds?

2. How deep should you plant the seeds?

3. How long will it take for the seeds to germinate (sprout)?

4. When can you harvest the seeds?

5. In what kind of weather do radish plants grow best?

6. Do radish plants like sun or shade?

7. What does the symbol [▦] stand for on the map?

8. Find your state on the map. What are the best months for planting radish seeds outdoors?

EXTENSION Have students use the information on their seed packages to plant their radish seeds. Provide rulers to determine planting depth. Encourage students to use their Science Journals to record observations about the radishes' progress.

LITERATURE CONNECTION

The Tale of Peter Rabbit by Beatrix Potter makes a delightful introduction or conclusion to activities on seeds. Students enjoy this classic story of the naughty rabbit who sneaked into Mr. McGregor's garden and ate too many radishes.

RADISH SEEDS

	Plant Spacing	Planting Depth	Days to Germination	Days to Harvest
Row:	10 in.	1/2 in.	4 to 6	25
Plant:	1 in.			

Radishes grow best in cool weather. Look at the map to find your state. It will show you the best time to plant radish seeds outdoors. Radish plants grow best in a sunny spot. Radishes can also be grown indoors in a sunny window. Water them when the soil feels dry. Radishes are tasty with vegetable dip or to spice up a salad.

When to Plant Outdoors:

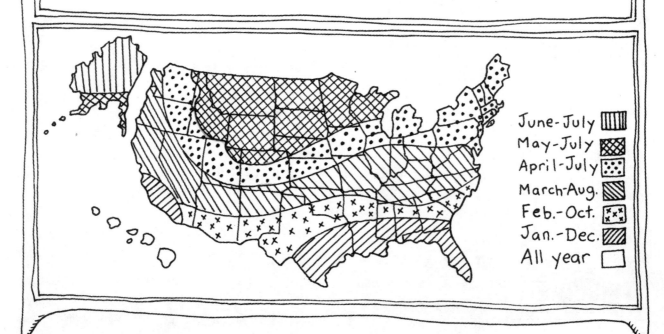

June-July
May-July
April-July
March-Aug.
Feb.-Oct.
Jan.-Dec.
All year

Seed Snack

Celebrate your seed study with a delicious and healthy seed snack. With the exception of water and salt, each ingredient in this granola recipe comes from a seed or plant. Discuss the ingredients and their sources as students prepare the recipe.

INGREDIENTS

6 cups oats

2 cups wheat germ

2 cups toasted sunflower seeds

1 cup toasted sesame seeds

1/2 cup flour

2 cups brown sugar

1 cup water

1 cup corn oil

2 teaspoons salt

2 tablespoons vanilla

1 cup raisins, dried cranberries, or other dried fruits

WHAT TO DO

Mix all the ingredients. Spread the ingredients on two cookie sheets. Bake at 350° F for 30 minutes. Stir occasionally while baking. After these ingredients are baked, add raisins, dried cranberries, or other dried fruit if desired. Serve in cups. (Makes about 12 to 14 cups.)

INTERACTIVE BULLETIN BOARD

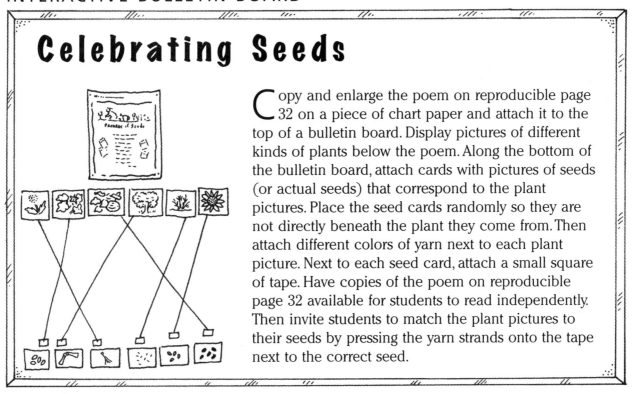

Celebrating Seeds

Copy and enlarge the poem on reproducible page 32 on a piece of chart paper and attach it to the top of a bulletin board. Display pictures of different kinds of plants below the poem. Along the bottom of the bulletin board, attach cards with pictures of seeds (or actual seeds) that correspond to the plant pictures. Place the seed cards randomly so they are not directly beneath the plant they come from. Then attach different colors of yarn next to each plant picture. Next to each seed card, attach a small square of tape. Have copies of the poem on reproducible page 32 available for students to read independently. Then invite students to match the plant pictures to their seeds by pressing the yarn strands onto the tape next to the correct seed.

Package of Seeds

They can't see their pictures,
they can't read the label—
the seeds in a package—
so how are they able
to know if they're daisies
or greens for the table?
It sounds like a fancy,
it sounds like a fable,
but you do the sowing,
the weeding, the hoeing,
and they'll do the knowing
of how to be growing.

—Aileen Fisher

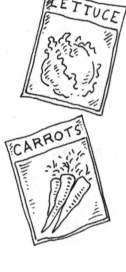

CHAPTER FOUR

GERMINATION

Germination is where it all begins, when a seed starts its life and the transformation into a plant.

Sprout It Out

Large dried lima beans make wonderful first-time sprouters. They are fast germinators and grow long, thick white sprouts that are easy to handle and measure.

MATERIALS
- ❊ for each student: plastic sandwich bag that zips closed; three dried lima beans, soaked overnight; wet paper towel; Science Journal
- ❊ for the class: stapler; masking tape or small stick-on notepads; markers

SAFETY TIP *Make sure students understand that they shouldn't put their fingers in their eyes or mouths after handling their seeds.*

WHAT TO DO

1 Pass out the bags and seeds. Show children how to fold a paper towel in half and place it in the bag. You or another adult should add the water/bleach solution to moisten the paper towel. (See Teacher Tip.)

TEACHER TIP
To prevent the lima bean seeds from becoming moldy in the bags, add a tablespoon of household bleach to a gallon of water. You or another adult should use this solution to moisten the paper towels students put in their bags.

2 Next, have students put a line of staples across the bag about 2 inches from the bottom. The staples will keep the beans in place. Then they place the lima beans in the bag and seal it.

3 Have children use tape or stick-on notes to label their bags with their names and place them in a dark spot such as a closet or inside a desk. Encourage students to record in their Science Journals what they have done so far and to note their observations throughout the rest of the activity.

4 Keep the seed bags in a dark place until the first sign of green appears. Check to make sure the paper towels stay moist.

5 Once the seeds sprout, tape the bags to a window where they will get plenty of sun.

Critical Thinking Questions

ASK: *Which part of the seed grows first?*

What happens to the seed coat as the seed sprouts?

Why is one part growing down?

What is that part called?

Does it matter what way the seed was placed in the bag?

EXTENSIONS

✻ Some students may ask questions that can be answered through experimentation. Possible questions might include: Will a seed grow without its coat? Will a seed grow without its cotyledon? Encourage groups of interested students to set up experiments to find the answers and report to the class. Student-generated questions provide valuable opportunities to discuss how experiments can be set up to help find answers.

✻ Have students turn their observations into data by using measurement. Students will increase the accuracy of their sprout observations by using pieces of yarn or string and rulers as measuring tools. They can make simple graphs of their sprouts' stem and root growth rates by gluing the yarn pieces side by side into their Science Journals. Then, using rulers, they can record the length of each piece.

Sprouting Groups

In this set of experiments, students test the sprouting success of seeds using the variables of light, moisture, temperature, and air.

MATERIALS

❋ plastic sandwich bags that zip closed, dried lima beans, paper towels, water/bleach solution (see page 33), masking tape or small stick-on notes, rulers, Science Journals

WHAT TO DO

1 Divide the class into groups and have each group choose one of the following questions (or have students come up with their own to test).

❋ Do lima bean seeds sprout better in the light or in the dark?

❋ Do lima bean seeds sprout better in cold or warm temperatures?

❋ Do lima bean seeds sprout better when wet or dry?

❋ Will frozen lima bean seeds sprout? How about seeds that have been boiled?

2 Give each group 8 seeds, plastic bags, and paper towels. Explain that the groups must decide how to set up an experiment to answer their question. Allow time for students to think of ideas and, if necessary, provide some coaching. Discuss the importance of testing only one variable (a condition that changes) at a time.

3 Once each group has made a plan, have students divide up the responsibilities. Jobs might include labeling the bags, inserting the seeds, sealing the bags, and placing them in the appropriate location. You or another adult should moisten any paper towels that need to be moistened.

4 Have students describe their experiment in their Science Journals. You might provide copies of the Science Journal reproducible (page 8) for this purpose.

5 Have each group check their bags every other day and record observations and sprout-growth measurements on simple charts.

6 After two weeks, have students write a conclusion based on their findings. Then invite the groups to share the results of their investigations with the class. Make a class chart that summarizes students' discoveries. Encourage students to evaluate the steps of their experiment and to indicate what they felt worked well and what they would do differently the next time. (In general, students will discover that seeds will not usually sprout without water or in cold temperatures. Light is not needed for a seed to germinate. In fact, seeds kept in the dark sprout faster.)

What Do Roots and Stems Do?

As students plant seeds, they will discover that seeds grow in two directions, developing both roots and stems. To demonstrate the major role that these plant parts play, have students conduct the following experiments. Begin by explaining that roots and stems are important plant parts. On the blackboard or a chart, list these functions:

ROOTS	STEMS
Store food	Hold up leaves and flowers
Hold plant in place in the earth	Carry food and water to plant parts
Take in minerals and water from the soil	

ROOTS

MATERIALS

❀ for each student: plastic sandwich bag that zips closed; 3 dried lima beans, soaked overnight; paper towel; three small objects (birthday candle, Lego block, rubber band, paper clip, pen cap); Science Journal

❀ for the class: water/bleach solution (see page 33); masking tape or small stick-on notepads; hand lenses

WHAT TO DO

1 To help students investigate how roots help hold a plant in place, have them each set up a seed bag as described in Sprout It Out (page 33). This time, however, don't put a line of staples across the bag. Then have students find three small objects to put in the bag. Tell them to put these in the bag where they think the roots will grow. Students then seal the bags and hang them in a place that will get sun.

2 Encourage students to observe changes in the bags for about five to seven days. Hand lenses will help them observe tiny root hairs. Guide students to observe what the roots do as they grow (hold onto the object, grow around it or inside it). Have them record and draw their observations in their Science Journals.

3 Help students apply what they've learned. Have them look at the list on the blackboard again and ask: How might roots underground help a plant? (Help anchor it in the soil; grow around rocks or other obstacles.)

STEMS

MATERIALS ✼ different kinds of plant stems (pumpkin stem, rhubarb, sugarcane, asparagus stalks, as well as celery stalks); sharp knife; tall clear jars; blue food coloring; hand lenses; Science Journals

WHAT TO DO

1 Help students investigate what's inside stems that help plants grow. Cut off the ends of the stems so students can see the structures within. Divide the class into groups and hand out samples of the different stems and hand lenses.

2 Encourage students to use hand lenses to look inside each stem. Have them draw pictures in their Science Journals showing how the different stems look inside, and label each one with the plant it comes from.

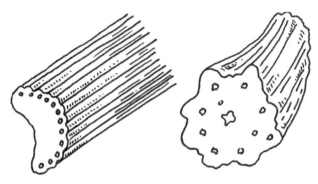

Celery stalk   Pumpkin stem

3 Ask: What do you see inside that might help these plants grow? (Though the inside of each stem may vary somewhat, students should be able to observe a ring of dots set in fibrous material. The dots are the stem's pipes. They work like a circulatory system, moving water up and down the stem to plant parts such as leaves and roots. If students have difficulty seeing the dots, the next part of the activity will help.)

4 Hand out a jar of water to each group and add a few drops of food coloring. Tell students to place their celery stalks and other stems in the colored water. Ask each group to predict and record in their Science Journals what will happen.

5 Let the stalks sit in the water overnight. Then have students check them for changes. (As the pipes within the stalks take up the colored water, the stalks become bluish.)

6 Have students use hand lenses to examine the ends of the stalks again. The food coloring should make the plant pipes easier to see.

7 Ask students to look again at the list on the blackboard and identify the function they have just demonstrated (to carry food, water, and/or minerals).

EXTENSION Many of the stems in this activity are foods (celery, asparagus, rhubarb, sugarcane). Bring in examples of foods that are roots (radishes, carrots, beets, turnips). Mix them up and challenge students to classify the foods as either roots or stems. Have them explain their reasoning.

Diary of a Seed

In this activity children create a paper model of an imaginary plant emerging from a seed. At the same time they write a diary of the seed's progress.

MATERIALS ❀ colored construction paper, glue, yarn, scissors, Science Journals

WHAT TO DO •

1 **Art:** Have students cut a large seed shape from a piece of 8-by-12-inch colored construction paper. **Writing:** Encourage children to begin the diaries of their seed in their Science Journals. This entry might describe what the seed is like (size, shape, texture).

2 **Art:** Ask students to pretend that their seed has sprouted. Have them cut lengths of yarn to glue to the seed for roots. Students can then cut a stem from construction paper and glue it to the seed. Suggest that they consult pictures or live plants to make their roots and stems look authentic. **Writing:** Have students continue with the diary, explaining what has happened.

3 **Art:** Students can finish their plants by cutting out leaves and large flowers from colored paper and attaching them to the stem. Display pictures to show the amazing variety of leaves and flowers found in nature. **Writing:** Ask students to describe in their Science Journals how their plant grows and blossoms. You might also challenge them to write about what will happen next to the plants.

TEACHER TIP
Display students' plants and diaries on a bulletin board so that the rest of the class can enjoy them.

LITERATURE CONNECTIONS

❀ For a larger-than-life story about plants, read *The Plant That Ate the Dirty Socks* by Nancy McArthur. This is the first in a series of books about two large plants with personalities.

❀ Children will also enjoy the exaggeration in *Grandpa's Too-Good Garden* by James Stevenson.

❀ In *The Big Seed* by Ellen Howard, a little girl is eager to see what grows from the big seed she plants.

❀ What happens when giant vegetable seedlings are sent aloft? Students can find out in the fantasy story, *June 29, 1999* by David Wiesner.

An Amazing Act

Chlorophyll (KLOR-uh-fil) is what makes leaves green. Chlorophyll is very important in a plant. It uses three things to make food:

1. energy from the **sun,**

2. a gas called **carbon dioxide** (KAR-buhn dye-OHK-side) from the air,

3. water.

Imagine if you had chlorophyll in your skin. You would sit in the sun when you were hungry!

Besides making food for itself, a plant also gives off **oxygen** (OHK-suh-juhn). All living things need oxygen.

Plants use sunlight, carbon dioxide, and water to make food and oxygen. This is called **photosynthesis** (foh-toh-SIN-thuh-siss). Scientists are trying to understand how plants do this amazing act.

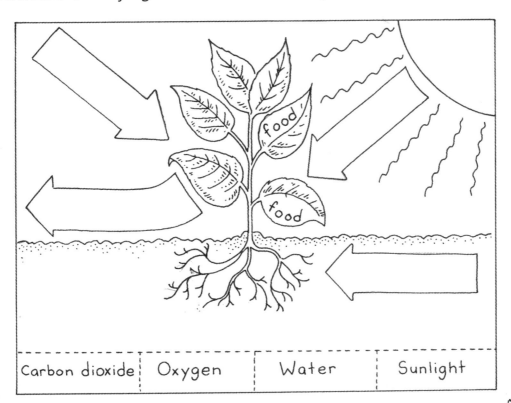

| Carbon dioxide | Oxygen | Water | Sunlight |

45

It's a Plant Thing

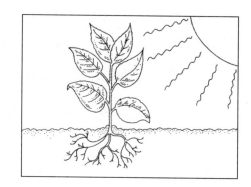

Characters: Plant
                       Student
                       Carbon dioxide
                       Sun
                       Water
                       Oxygen

Props: green tag-board LEAVES; yellow tag-board SUN; tag-board signs: OXYGEN, WATER, CARBON DIOXIDE, FOOD

Plant is onstage looking tired, arms with leaves hanging at sides. Student enters and looks plant over.

Student: You don't look very good.

Plant: I don't feel very good.

Student: What's wrong?

Plant: I don't ask for much. I'm easy to get along with. I don't pick on anyone. I just sit in my pot minding my own business.

Student: But why do you look so droopy?

Plant: Droopy? You're right. I'm very droopy. I can barely lift my leaves. Not that there's anything to lift them up for. Do you get my point?

Student: Ah, no.

Plant: Sunlight, my friend. I need to catch some rays. I can't go on without that solar power. It starts my day so I can photosynthesize.

Student: What's that?

Plant: I'll show you. Hey, airhead! [*Enter Carbon Dioxide holding up its sign.*] This is Carbon Dioxide, which I need to breathe. Now if you would kindly open that window... [*Sun enters holding cardboard sun.*] There now, I only need one more thing.

Student: What's that?

Plant: Water! [*Water enters holding up its sign.*]

Student: So?

Plant: Just wait. Now it's time to do my thing. [*Lifts leaves as if conducting music. Water, Carbon Dioxide, and Sun walk around in a circle.*] Now I can get what I need—food! [*Water, Carbon Dioxide and Sun come together and hold up food sign.*]

Water, Carbon Dioxide, Sun: Yummy plant food!

Student: Is that it?

Plant: No! You get something you need, too.

Oxygen: [*Steps forward holding its sign.*] You get oxygen— just what you need for a breath of fresh air!

Plant: And that, my friend, is photosynthesis!

Student: Amazing! Can I make food and oxygen that way?

Plant: Sorry! It's a plant thing.

The End

47

Leaf Covers

This experiment helps students discover what happens to chlorophyll when a leaf is kept from sunlight.

MATERIALS ❋ black construction paper, tape, live plants, Science Journals

WHAT TO DO . . . .

1 Have students fold and tape black paper envelopes to slip over sample leaves of classroom or school yard plants.

2 Ask children to predict what might happen to these leaves when they don't get sunlight. Have students write both the question and their prediction in their Science Journals.

3 Have each student place an envelope over a leaf either in the classroom or on the school grounds.

4 After five days, ask students to remove their envelopes. Ask: *How do the leaves you covered compare to the rest of the leaves on the plant?* (The green will have faded.)

5 Have students write in their Science Journals conclusions about what happened.

Out Comes the Oxygen

This activity demonstrates for students that plants release oxygen during photosynthesis.

MATERIALS ❈ tall narrow jar such as one olives come in; aquatic plant found in a pond or lake, or purchased from an aquarium supply store; large clear bowl of water; Science Journals

WHAT TO DO

1 Review with the class what the term photosynthesis means. Ask students to explain what a plant needs for photosynthesis to take place.

2 Remind students that air is invisible. Then explain that this demonstration will show oxygen in the form of bubbles coming from a plant during photosynthesis.

3 Tip the narrow jar under the water in the bowl so that it fills with water, then hold the jar upside down.

4 Slip the plant into the upside-down jar.

5 Place the bowl with the upside-down jar in sunlight.

6 After an hour, have students look for bubbles along the edges of leaves and at the water's surface. If necessary, leave the plant in the sunlight longer and check for bubbles every 30 minutes or so.

7 Have children draw pictures and write in their Science Journals descriptions of what happened.

Critical Thinking Questions

ASK: *Do you think there would be bubbles if the plant were kept in the dark?*

How could we help the plant to make more bubbles?

How do water plants help other living things in the lake or pond?

Very Vein

Leaves have veins that can be seen and felt. In this activity students discover that the purpose of these veins is not so different from the purpose of their own.

MATERIALS ❀ tissue paper, newsprint or other thin paper at least 8 1/2-by-11-inches, fresh leaves, crayons with paper wrappers removed

WHAT TO DO . . . .

1 Give each student a leaf. Have students close their eyes and rub their fingertips over the leaf surface to feel the veins.

2 Show students how to make rubbings of the veins by placing one half of a piece of tissue paper over a leaf, vein-side-up, and rubbing with the side of a crayon. The veins will appear as darker lines.

3 Direct students to look for veins in their own hands. Ask how their veins are similar to and different from a leaf's. Explain that a leaf's veins are used to carry water and food to the rest of the plant, and that human veins carry blood with the fluids and oxygen needed for life.

4 Conclude the activity by having children trace their own hand and draw how their veins look on the other half of the paper.

EXTENSION Collect students' leaf-vein rubbings and the leaves they used. Challenge students to see how many rubbings they can match up with the real leaves.

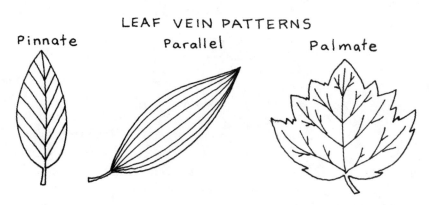

LEAF VEIN PATTERNS

Pinnate   Parallel   Palmate

CHAPTER SIX

FLOWERS

Flowers are the plant parts that people notice most. However, many people are not aware of the reason that plants display their bright petals. These activities help children learn to take a closer look at the flower as a seed maker.

Flower Parts

In this activity students learn the parts of a flower by taking one apart.

MATERIALS

❀ large simple flowers such as tulips, apple blossoms, or lilies; scissors; paste; tape; Parts of a Flower reproducible (page 53); Science Journals

WHAT TO DO

· ·

1 Give each student a copy of the Parts of a Flower reproducible and a flower. Allow time for students to examine their flowers and compare their appearance, scent, and texture with classmates' flowers.

2 Identify the petals. Ask: *What do you think the petals do?* Guide students to understand that the petals protect the other flower parts. The bright colors of the petals also attract insects such as bees and butterflies, and they in turn help the flower make new seeds through a process called *pollination*. Have students count and remove petals on their flowers. Ask: *Are all the petals the same color? Do all flowers have the same number of petals? Are all petals the same shape?* Have students compare their flowers with those of their classmates. Then have them draw and record their observations in their Science Journals. Students can also tape the petals into their notebooks, covering them with tape to protect them.

TEACHER TIP
Often florists provide slightly aged flowers for educational purposes at no charge.

3 Then ask students to locate the petals of the flower on the reproducible. Ask them to cut out the correct label and paste it on the diagram.

4 Next, students identify the *stamens*. Proceed in the same way, explaining that stamens make *pollen*. Pollen is a powder that a flower needs in order to make seeds. Pollen sticks to the tips, or *anthers*, of the stamens. Have students locate and count the stamens on their flowers.

Demonstrate how to rub a fingertip or a small paintbrush over the tips of the stamens to detect pollen. Have students rub a bit of the pollen on a page in their Science Journals, cover with tape, and label. Then have them remove the stamens from their flower and add them to their journals in the same manner.

5 Instruct students to locate the stamens of the flower on the reproducible. Ask them to cut out the correct label and paste it on the diagram.

6 Identify the *pistil* on a flower. Explain that when insects visit flowers, they help spread pollen. Have students find the pistil on their flowers and feel the top to see if it is sticky. Explain that the pollen sticks to the pistil, then travels down the tube to the bulging part that is called the *ovary*. There the pollen helps to make the plant's seeds. Have students remove the pistil and pull apart the ovary. Inside they may be able to see the tiny *ovules* that contain the eggs. Again share and compare discoveries, and allow students time to record their observations and add the plant parts to their journals.

7 Have students locate the pistil and ovary on the reproducible. Ask them to cut out the correct labels and add them to the diagram. You may wish to have students add these pages to their Science Journals.

Critical Thinking Questions

ASK: *How do petals help a flower?*

In what ways could pollen travel to the pistil?

Do all plants make flowers?

What happens to the rest of the flower after the petals fall off?

Why don't plants have flowers all the time?

Paper-Flower Models

Students can review what they have learned about flower parts as they make imaginary flowers!

MATERIALS ❈ florist's foam; small tin cans; green tomato sticks or wooden dowels, painted green; 1-inch Styrofoam balls; cotton swabs; 3-by-5-inch index cards; brightly colored construction paper; scissors; glue

WHAT TO DO . . . .

1 Provide each student with a can and enough florist's foam to cover the bottom. Explain that these will be the flowerpot and soil. Suggest that students cover the outside of their containers with colorful paper.

2 Have students cut leaf shapes from green paper and glue these onto a stick to form the leaves and stem of their flower. Students can set the stems into their containers.

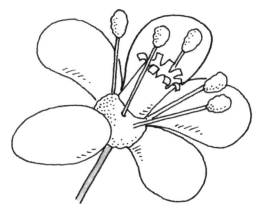

3 Show students how to cut an index card in half along the width, then roll and glue it into a tube. When the glue is dry, cut fringes on one end of the tube and roll the pieces back into curls. Put glue on the other end of the tube and stick it into the Styrofoam ball. This is the pistil.

4 Next, students paint the cotton swabs yellow. Show them how to put glue on the stick end of the swab and poke it into the Styrofoam ball to be a stamen. Have students make five stamens for their flower.

5 Students can design flower petals any way they choose. Have them cut five or more petals from colored paper. Remind them that the petals should be large to fit with the rest of the flower. Help students arrange their petals around the outside of the stamens and glue them to the Styrofoam ball.

6 Model how to carefully stick a flower onto its stem in the container. Have students group their flower pots together to make a colorful garden!

Pollination

Flowers are not only pretty to look at but also have an important function for the plant. Probing for pollen shows students where the working part of the flower begins.

MATERIALS ❄ cotton balls, construction paper scraps, glue, a variety of flowers

WHAT TO DO

1 Review what pollen is and that it is located on the tips (anthers) of a plant's stamens.

2 Give each student a cotton ball and construction paper scraps to make a bee. Students can cut out tiny features and glue them onto the cotton ball to make bee faces and antennae (see illustration). Explain that a real bee picks up pollen on the hairs of its legs while students' bees will pick up pollen on their cotton bodies. Insects collect nectar from the flower as they pollinate it. Bees turn this nectar into honey. (You'll find a honey-tasting activity on page 57.)

3 Provide students with flowers (or take them on a flower walk) and show them how to sweep their bees across the stamens to detect pollen.

4 At this time, you may wish to point out to students that all plants except fungi (mushrooms), ferns, and mosses produce flowers. Suggest that students look at shrubs, trees, and grasses to see what kinds of flowers they produce.

Critical Thinking Questions

ASK: *Which plants had the most pollen?*

Why might some flowers have more pollen than others?

Were any unusual flowers found?

Did anyone feel sticky nectar on a flower?

Did anyone see insects pollinating the flowers?

LITERATURE CONNECTION
Share the book *Dancers in the Garden* by Joanne Ryder, a story about how hummingbirds pollinate flowers.

Honey Tasting

Students will have a sweet time at a honey-tasting party.

MATERIALS ❊ honey from different types of flowers, bread or crackers

WHAT TO DO

1 Display different kinds of honey. Hold them up to the light so students can compare their color. Invite students to sniff them to compare their scents.

2 Spread the different kinds of honey on small pieces of bread and invite students to sample them and compare the flavors.

TEACHER TIP
If possible, arrange for a beekeeper to visit the classroom to talk about this fascinating work. To locate someone in your area, write or call:
American Beekeeping Federation
P.O. Box 1038
Jessup, GA 31598
(912) 427-4233.

Flower Scents

Capture flower fragrances by making potpourri in the classroom.

MATERIALS ❊ an old window screen; flower petals; spices such as cinnamon, mint, cloves, and marjoram; plastic bags that seal; small, clear plastic containers or netting; ribbon; My Potpourri Recipe reproducible (page 59)

WHAT TO DO

1 Have students collect scented flower petals to bring to school. Suggest petals from roses, lilacs, honeysuckle, apple blossoms, lily of the valley, or peonies. You might also contact local florists for donations of old flowers.

2 Spread the petals on a window screen supported by two boards, or between two chairs. Choose a warm place, not in direct sunlight, that is out of busy traffic patterns. Ask volunteers to turn the petals regularly as they dry out over the next few weeks.

3 As the petals become dry and brittle, store them in sealed plastic bags.

4 When enough petals have been dried, give each student a third of a cup of petals. Invite students to choose the spices they wish to add. Caution that students only need a few pinches of a spice.

5 Pass out the My Potpourri Recipe reproducible and have students fill it in to describe the ingredients and steps they used to make their potpourri.

6 Students can put their potpourri in clear containers or pieces of netting tied into sachets. Help children tie their containers with bright ribbon. Invite students to decide what to do with their potpourri—give as gifts, donate to a school fair, or sell to raise money for a favorite cause. Don't forget to save one container for your classroom!

Critical Thinking Questions

ASK: *What kinds of flowers have the strongest scent?*

Is it only the petals of a plant that smell?

What parts of the plant does each of the spices come from?

Why do the petals shrink?

LITERATURE CONNECTION

Rose in My Garden by Arnold Lobel is a good book for reading and learning flower names. Try using the book as a choral reading activity so students can appreciate the rhythm and pattern created with flower names.

Name _____

My Potpourri Recipe

My Potpourri Recipe

Ingredients_____

_____

Steps_____

_____

_____

Results _____

_____

_____

Made by_____

Wildflower Alert

Contact your state department of natural resources or department of environmental protection for a list of protected wildflowers in your area. Ask for assistance in finding slides or pictures of these flowers.

MATERIALS

❋ list of protected wildflowers for your state; pictures of these wildflowers; rulers and yardsticks; My Wildflower Chart reproducible (page 61); clipboards or thin, hardcover books and binder clips

WHAT TO DO

TEACHER TIPS
The National Audubon Society Pocket Guide to Familiar Flowers of North America, by Region *(Alfred Knopf, 1996)* and Peterson's First Guide to Wildflowers *(Houghton Mifflin, 1987) are two excellent field guides to wildflowers.*

1 Display samples or pictures of garden flowers and nonprotected wildflowers. Discuss where each might grow. Point out that although people plant some flowers in gardens, and other flowers grow wild, all flowers start from seeds.

2 Discuss what happens to a plant when a flower is picked. Ask: *Is the plant able to make seeds? What happens if too many flowers are picked or pulled up by their roots? Why are seeds important?* Compare the difference in picking flowers from a garden to picking those in the wild.

3 Show pictures of rare or endangered wildflowers. Discuss why some flowers are endangered. Ask: *Why is it important not to pick these flowers? How can people help protect these plants?*

4 If possible, invite a naturalist to talk to your class about wildflowers. Or take a field trip to a nature center where students can see and identify wildflowers. Beforehand, pass out multiple copies of the My Wildflower Chart reproducible to each student. Have students attach them to clipboards if available (or attach them to a thin, hardcover book with a binder clip). Students can take these along and fill them out on the walk. Have a field guide to wildflowers on hand to help students identify their finds.

5 Conclude by asking students to make posters with pictures of endangered wildflowers. Have students think of slogans that would encourage people to protect wildflowers.

Showy Lady's Slipper

White Milkweed

Indian Paintbrush

Fringed Gentian

Name _____

My Wildflower Chart

Number of flowers on stem? _____

Is the flower alone or with lots of others? _____

Where did you find it? _____

How big is the flower? _____

How high is it off the ground? _____

What does it smell like? _____

Draw the leaf shape:

What color(s) is the flower? _____

How many pistils does it have? _____

How many stamens does it have? _____

How many petals does it have? _____

What is the flower's name? _____

Draw the flower:

CHAPTER SEVEN

FRUITS

As the ovary of a flower matures, it becomes a fruit—a fleshy structure that contains seeds.

Fruit Find

Many things people call vegetables are really fruits. In this activity students identify foods that scientists classify as fruits.

MATERIALS   ❋ assortment of fruit and nonfruit foods, knife, How Does a Pumpkin Grow? reproducible (page 63), scissors, stapler, Science Journals

WHAT TO DO   ·

1 To help the class understand how fruits develop, pass out copies of the How Does a Pumpkin Grow? reproducible and have students make mini-books. Tell them that the pages are all mixed up. Ask students to number the pages from 1 to 7, then cut them apart and put them in the right order. To make their book, they put the cover on top and staple the pages together. After students read their books, talk about the importance of fruits as part of a healthy diet.

2 Have student write or draw in their Science Journals a list of favorite fruits.

3 Point out that some foods are often called vegetables but they are really fruits because they contain seeds. Hold up different plant products and ask students to decide if each is a fruit. Examples of fruits to use are a peach, a pear, a banana, a melon, a squash, a pumpkin, a tomato, a green pepper, and a cucumber. Nonfruits could include a potato, a carrot, an onion, a lima bean, and a shelled pea. To help students decide, cut open the foods to look for seeds.

> ### Critical Thinking Questions
>
> ASK: *Why do plants have fruits?*
>
> *Why do you think people have trouble calling foods like tomatoes and cucumbers fruits?*

Name _____

Grocery Store Fruit Finders

Find as many of these fruits and fruit products that you can.
Check each item that you find. What other fruit products can you
add to the list?

☐ orange

☐ mango

☐ papaya

☐ avocado

☐ canned plums

☐ grapefruit juice

☐ lemon gelatin dessert

☐ raisin bran cereal

☐ frozen cherries

☐ frozen lemonade

☐ blueberry toaster pastries

☐ prunes

☐ fig cookies

☐ strawberry yogurt

☐ grape jelly

☐ lime sherbet

_____

_____

_____

_____

65

Dried Apple Rings

A study of fruit is not complete without a taste of it. Try making this simple snack of apple rings.

MATERIALS ❋ a dozen fresh, firm apples; string; vegetable peeler; paring knife; cheesecloth; Science Journals

WHAT TO DO

1 Peel and core the apples beforehand. Then cut them crosswise into 1/8- to 1/4-inch-thick rings.

2 Have students work in groups to slide the apple rings onto string.

3 Hang the string horizontally in a warm, dry spot. Tying the ends of the string to two chair backs and pulling the string taut works well. To protect the fruit from dust and insects, drape cheesecloth over the rings.

4 Have volunteers check the apples once a week to see if they are leathery. This should take several weeks indoors. (If you dry the apple rings outside, they will be ready in just a few days.)

5 Have students record in their Science Journals. Encourage them to use descriptive words to compare a fresh apple slice (white, wet, juicy, crunchy) with a dried one (brown, shriveled, dry, sweeter, chewy).

6 Serve the dried apples as a snack along with apples in another form such as juice or cider.

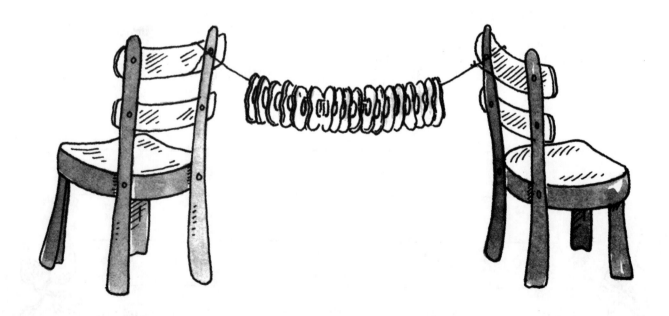

Fruit Fact Riddles

Finding facts through research gives students an opportunity to learn more about a favorite fruit. In this activity, they will present their facts in riddle form.

MATERIALS ❋ construction paper, crayons or colored markers, books for research (see Classroom Resources, page 71)

WHAT TO DO

1 Compile a list of fruits on the blackboard. Have students choose one fruit to research. Each child should have a different fruit.

2 Pass out paper that has been folded in half. Explain that students are to write a riddle about their fruit on the outside, then draw a picture of it inside. For example, the riddles might give clues about the size, shape, name, or color of a fruit; the kind of plant it grows on; the kind of flower it grows from; how the fruit is eaten; whether animals eat the fruit; where the fruit grows. You may wish to share sample riddles as models: *What fruit looks like a yellow smile?* (a banana) *This fruit isn't beautiful. What is it?* (an ugly fruit) *I'm round and red and people often think I'm a vegetable. What am I?* (a tomato).

3 Direct students to the resource books in your classroom or school library. Mention that they might also obtain information in a local produce store.

4 When students have completed their research and riddles, have them take turns reading the riddles aloud for the class to guess.

5 Collect the riddle pages and staple them together into a classroom book.

EXTENSION Have students cut out small paper fruit shapes and attach them to a large world map to show the places where they grow.

CHAPTER EIGHT

WRAP-UP

Celebration Day!

Ending a unit with a celebration reinforces for children the idea that learning is important and worth recognition. Here are a few ideas to use in a special culminating event—a plant party.

Invitations Children will enjoy making and sending invitations to parents and family members for a Plant Party. Try creating these with pressed flowers (see the activity on page 54) or leaf prints (see the activity on page 43).

Displays Invite children to help plan how to set up the classroom to show off their completed projects. Suggest that students make special signs or labels for the

plants they grew. Display any charts, research, books, posters, collections, and artwork that students completed during the unit. Projects might include the paper-clip tree (see page 27), the leaf-print banners (see page 43), the paper-flower models (see page 55), and students' Science Journals.

Plant Snacks Serve refreshments made from plants, such as fruit juice, vegetable or herb dip, fruit and honey dip, or alfalfa sprouts and peanut butter on whole-grain crackers (see page 39). You might also serve a seed snack (see page 31) or dried apple rings (see page 66).

Entertainment Students might plan to put on a production of the skit "It's a Plant Thing" (see pages 46-47). You could also invite your class to label plants found on school grounds (students can make plant markers by cutting up clean,

Classroom Resources

LITERATURE

Backyard Sunflower by Elizabeth King; Dutton, 1993

Bean Boy by George Shannon; Greenwillow Books, 1984

The Big Seed by Ellen Howard; Simon & Schuster, 1993

City Green by Dyanne DiSalvo-Ryan; Morrow Junior Books, 1994

Daisy's Garden by Mordecai Gerstein; Hyperion Books, 1995

Dancers in the Garden by Joanne Ryder; Sierra Club, 1992

Dinosaur Garden by Liza Donnelly; Scholastic, 1990

Grandpa's Too-Good Garden by James Stevenson;
    Greenwillow Books, 1989

The Great Pumpkin Switch by Megan McDonald; Orchard Books, 1992

Growing Vegetable Soup by Lois Ehlert; Harcourt Brace, 1987

How a Shirt Grew in the Fields by Marguerita Rudolph; Clarion, 1992

John Chapman: The Man Who Was Johnny Appleseed by Carol
    Greene; Children's Press, 1991

June 29, 1999 by David Wiesner; Clarion, 1992

The Lotus Seed by Sherry Garland; Harcourt Brace, 1993

My Garden by Arnold Lobel; Lothrop, Lee & Shepard, 1990

Pierrot's ABC Garden by Anita Lobel; Western Publishing, 1992

The Plant that Ate the Dirty Socks by Nancy McArthur;
    Avon Books, 1988

Planting a Rainbow by Lois Ehlert; Harcourt Brace Jovanovich, 1988

The Popcorn Book by Tomie de Paola; Holiday House, 1978

The Pumpkin Man and the Crafty Creeper by Margaret Mahy;
    Lothrop, Lee & Shepard, 1990

Pumpkins: A Story for a Field by Mary Lyn Ray; Harcourt Brace, 1992

Queen Anne's Lace by Jerome Wexler; Whitman, 1994

Rose in My Garden by Arnold Lobel; Greenwillow, 1994

The Seasons of Arnold's Apple Tree by Gail Gibbons;
    Harcourt Brace, 1984

Seeds by George Shannon; Houghton Mifflin, 1994

Something Is Growing by Walter L. Krudop; Simon & Schuster, 1995

Sunflower by Miela Ford; Greenwillow, 1995

The Tale of Peter Rabbit by Beatrix Potter; Penguin Group, 1902 (1989)

The Tiny Seed by Eric Carle; Picture Book Studio, 1987

POETRY *Always Wondering* by Aileen Fisher; HarperCollins, 1991

The Earth Is Painted Green edited by Barbara Brenner; Scholastic, 1994

Everything Glistens and Everything Sings by Charlotte Zolotow; Harcourt Brace, 1987

The Tree by Judy Hindley; Clarkson N. Potter, 1990

NONFICTION *The Clover and the Bee: A Book of Pollination* by Anne O. Dowden; HarperCollins, 1990

Discovering Trees by Douglas Florian; Aladdin Books, 1990

Exploring Plants by Ed Catherall; Raintree, 1992

Eyewitness Plant by David Burnie; Alfred Knopf, 1989

From Flower to Flower: Animals and Pollination by Patricia Lauber; Crown, 1987

From Seed to Plant by Gail Gibbons; Holiday House, 1991

Get Growing by Lois Walker; John Wiley, 1991

How Seeds Travel by Cynthia Overbeck; Lerner, 1982

Look What I Did with a Leaf by Morteza E. Sohi; Walker and Company, 1993

National Audubon Society Pocket Guide to Familiar Flowers of North America, by Region, and *Familiar Trees of North America, by Region;* Alfred Knopf, 1996

Peterson First Guides: Trees and *Wildflowers* by Roger Tory Peterson; Houghton Mifflin, 1987

The Plant-and-Grow Project Book by Ulla Dietl; Sterling, 1994

Plant Experiments by Vera Webster; Childrens Press, 1982

Plant Families by Carol Lerner; Morrow Junior Books, 1989

Plants in Action by Robin Kerrod; Marshall Cavendish, 1989

The Reason for a Flower by Ruth Heller; Grosset & Dunlap, 1983

Seeds: Pop, Stick, Glide by Patricia Lauber; Crown, 1991

The Victory Garden Kids' Book by Marjorie Waters; Houghton Mifflin, 1988

SOURCES OF ORGANIC SEEDS

Organic Seed Suppliers:

Let's Get Growing; (800) 408-1868

Seeds of Change; (504) 438-8080